Where was Patrick Henry On the 29 th of May ?

by Jean Fritz

illustrated by Margot Tomes

PAPERSTAR

G. P. Putnam's Sons

The Putnam & Grosset Group

To Ferd, Margaret and Regina

Text copyright © 1975 by Jean Fritz
Illustrations copyright © 1975 by Margot Tomes
All rights reserved. This book, or parts thereof, may not be reproduced
in any form without permission in writing from the publisher.
PaperStar and G. P. Putnam's Sons are divisions of
The Putnam & Grosset Group,
200 Madison Avenue, New York, NY 10016.
PaperStar is a registered trademark of The Putnam Berkley Group, Inc.
The PaperStar logo is a trademark of The Putnam Berkley Group, Inc.
Originally published in 1975 by Coward McCann, Inc.
First PaperStar edition published in 1997
Published simultaneously in Canada
Printed in the United States of America
Library of Congress Catalog Card Number: 74-83014
ISBN 0-399-23305-9 (hardcover)
15 17 19 20 18 16
PaperStar ISBN 0-698-11439-6 (paperback)
3 5 7 9 10 8 6 4 2

THE FIRST CAPITOL AT WILLIAMSBURG   BUILT IN 1701-5
BURNED DOWN IN 1747

May 29th, 1736, was a good day to be alive in Virginia. Spring was spilling over into birdsong and the countryside was wild with flowers—daisies, bluebonnets, golden ragwort, purple vetch on the hillsides, blue-eyed grass in the crannies, pink dragon heads in the lowlands. The rivers rushed, slanting across the face of the land, picking up tributaries along the way and darting off into so many crooked creeks that the old maps look as if they had been drawn by men with unsteady hands carried away by love for Virginia. The names of the creeks are themselves a wonder: Hat Creek, Dog Creek, Sailors Creek, Bear Garden Creek, Skin Creek.

In 1736 Hanover County had 322 square miles of land, three large rivers, each with its brood of creeks, and 2,000 men over sixteen years old.

And it had Patrick Henry.

And where was Patrick on the 29th of May?

Well, he was in bed. Crying, most likely. Drowning out the birdsong. And why not? He had just been born and didn't know about the creeks and woodlands. He was too small to know a fox from a flower and too young to be counted when they added up the men in Virginia.

In a few years, of course, it would be different. Come a nice spring day with redbirds calling and Patrick would be off to the nearest creek, a fishing pole over his shoulder. (The creeks quivered with life in those days.

Bullheads, redeyes, flatbacks, rockfish—to mention only a few.) Or he'd be off to the woods, a gun in his hand and a dog or two at his heels. (There were still wolves in Hanover County when Patrick was young. And of course fox, deer, possum, coon and other game.)

Sometimes he would just go off. He'd mosey about, barefoot, through the woods or lie down by a creek and listen. Mostly to birdsong. He had the idea that if he listened long enough and hard enough, he'd be able to figure out what the birds were saying. Meanwhile he practiced imitating their songs so he'd be ready to talk back. He became so expert, he could not only imitate a mockingbird, he could imitate a mockingbird imitating a jay.

Patrick had other listening pleasures. The sound of rain on the roof was one. The long, low, lonesome faraway echo of his father's foxhorn. The bugling of the dogs on the trail. The sweet music of fiddles and flutes. (He taught himself to play the flute when he had to stay indoors with a broken collar bone.) The voice of his

Uncle Langloo Winston when he made a speech. On
Election Day, it was said, Langloo Winston would roll
his rich words into a crowd until he had the hair standing up on people's heads. (His uncle was also a famous
hunter and spent six months of the year hunting deer
and camping with Indians.)

It was a small, cheerful world that Patrick lived in with many pleasures, but school was not one of them. Patrick had, of course, to fit school into growing up, but he gave it no more attention than was necessary. Come a nice spring day with redbirds calling and he might not even make it to the schoolhouse door. But generally he was there, waiting for the day to end so he'd be free again, running barefoot and wild on the land. It was as if Patrick Henry had soaked up through the bottoms of his bare feet the two things that he prized most all his life—freedom and the good Virginia land. Not that he thought much about them. He took his days for granted and as for the future, he had no plans.

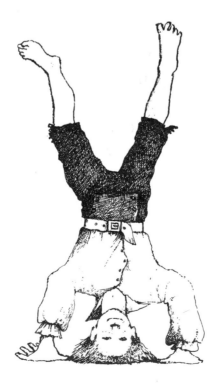

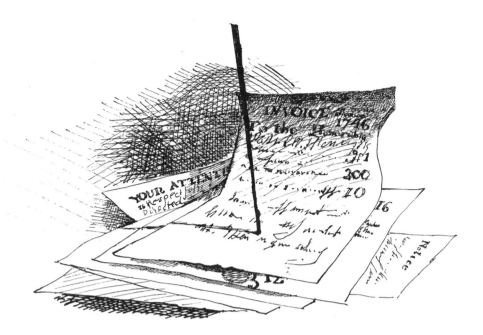

His father, on the other hand, gave Patrick's future considerable thought. John Henry was a planter, a surveyor, an officer in the Virginia militia, a justice in the county court, and one of the few men in Hanover County who had a university education, but he had a large family and money was a problem. By the time Patrick was fifteen, he had, in addition to his older brother William, seven younger sisters—all of whom would have to be supported until they were married and then, according to custom, they would have to be provided with substantial gifts of land or money. So of course William and Patrick were expected to go out in the world and make their own living as soon as they could. William, however, was so irresponsible as a young man that John Henry centered his hopes on Patrick.

But what was Patrick to do? Mr. Henry had taken him out of the local school when he was ten and opened his own school for about a dozen boys in the neighborhood. The next five years Patrick studied under his father —Latin, history, mathematics, and a smattering of Greek. The trouble was not that learning came hard to Patrick; he just didn't like to tie himself down to it. In short, he was no scholar.

Indeed, Patrick Henry didn't seem to have any particularly useful talents. Looking back on their boyhood together, one friend remembered that Patrick had been a practical joker. Several times when a group of boys had been out in a canoe together, the canoe had tipped over and after a while the boys noticed that every time this happened, they would all be fully dressed but Patrick would have his clothes off, ready for a swim.

Another friend recalled Patrick's underwear. No matter how sloppy Patrick's outer appearance, this friend said, his underwear was always clean. And when Patrick put on boots, he didn't do what his brother William did—just pull the boots on over his dirty bare feet. Patrick put on stockings first. But none of these habits was likely to help him earn a living. In fact, his friends agreed, there was nothing special about Patrick Henry as a boy. He had a happy disposition, he was fond of his gun, he had a nice ear for music, and he had a way of observing people closely. And, like his sister Elizabeth, he had what was called a "sending" voice; that is, he could send his voice out so that it could be heard clearly at a distance. But still he couldn't send his voice out and expect it to bring back a living.

On May 29th, 1752, Patrick became sixteen. He was six feet tall, a lanky, sharp-boned young man with flash-

ing blue eyes, generally dressed in checked breeches and a jumpshirt, generally in his bare feet. He was old enough now to be counted among the men in Virginia and old enough to make his own living. And where was he?

Well, he may have been stretched out on a sack of salt. People claimed this was Patrick's favorite resting place and he rested a good deal. His father had set up his two boys as storekeepers on the Pamunkey River, but William paid little attention to the store and although people came in to pass the time of day, they seldom put down hard cash for the goods they bought. Besides, the store wasn't always open. Come a nice spring day with redbirds calling and Patrick might be at the store and then again he might be down at the river or off in the woods. Or he might be across the county, courting. Patrick was sweet on young Sarah Shelton whose father operated a tavern at Hanover Courthouse.

As it turned out, Patrick's storekeeping was a failure but his courting was a success. When he was eighteen years old, he got rid of the store and married sixteen-year-old Sarah. As a wedding present, Sarah's father gave them six slaves and three hundred acres of land cut off from his own estate. So Patrick became a tobacco farmer. For three years he went through the business of planting, cultivating, leafing, worming, and curing tobacco, and then his house burned down and he gave up the farm.

He and Sarah moved to Hanover Courthouse and decided to give storekeeping another try, but when they
had only 26 customers in six months, they quit altogether. Patrick and Sarah had two children now,
Martha and John, but they had little else. They lived
with Sarah's father at the tavern and Patrick helped take
care of the guests, many of them lawyers and their
clients doing business at the courthouse across the
road. Patrick handed out refreshment, made friends,
and sometimes entertained guests with his fiddle.

At the quarter sessions of the court in March, June,
September, and December, the most important cases

were tried and then every bed in the tavern would be taken. (It cost 75¢ a night for a bed with clean sheets.) Traveling troupes of acrobats and jugglers came to town at that time; peddlers came to sell their wares; there were horse races, cockfights, and wrestling matches. From all over the county people came to see the shows, do their trading, and hear the cases argued.

Patrick attended court as often as possible. He liked to watch a lawyer run his opposition up a tree. He liked to listen to him roll out his words, the way his Uncle Langloo did on Election Day. The more he listened, the more he thought he might like to have a try at it himself. After all, he was twenty-four years old now; he no longer had a farm or a store or even a house. He had to try *something*. So he got a few books and began studying on his own.

This was the winter of 1760, about the same time as young seventeen-year-old Thomas Jefferson met him at a houseparty and was struck by Patrick's "passion for fiddling, dancing and pleasantry." But Patrick read at least two heavy law books that winter and in the middle of April he hung up a sign at John Shelton's tavern. *Patrick Henry*, the sign said, *Attorney at Law*. Patrick had been to Williamsburg, the capital of Virginia; he'd been examined by three prominent lawyers and he'd been issued a license to practice law. (He had also been told that he needed to study some more.)

In his first year Patrick represented 60 clients (many of them relatives) in 176 cases but the cases didn't amount to much and he collected less than half of what was owed him. Much of the time he had so little to do, he'd ride into the piney woods for a week or more of hunting—"sleeping under a tent," according to Thomas Jefferson, "wearing the same shirt the whole time." Then likely as not, he'd go directly to court in his greasy leather breeches and a pair of saddle bags on his arm.

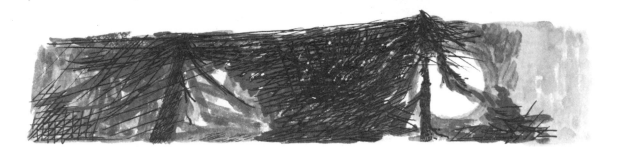

What Patrick Henry needed to prove himself as a lawyer was a big case at one of the quarter sessions of court when the whole county would take an interest.

At the December session in 1763 Patrick had his chance. There was an argument between a group of preachers (or parsons, as they were called) and the people, but in one sense it was an argument between the people of Virginia and England. For a long time England had been so busy fighting wars that she had left America relatively free to manage her own affairs. But now the French and Indian War was over, a new king was on the throne, and there were rumors that England had a plan to rule the colonies more strictly. With the Parsons' Case, it looked as if England had already started. The case went back to a year when the tobacco crop in Virginia failed. Instead of selling for the normal rate of 2 cents a pound, tobacco was so scarce, it sold for 6 cents. This should have been good news for the parsons because, according to law, they were paid in tobacco, but this year the people felt they couldn't afford it. So they passed a new law which allowed them to pay the parsons in cash at the 2 cent rate. The parsons took their case to the king; the king vetoed the law and now a group of parsons were suing the people for damages and back pay. And Patrick Henry was representing the people.

On the day of the trial Patrick was uneasy. Not only were there more spectators than he'd ever seen at the courthouse, there were two men that he wished were not there. The first was his Uncle Patrick who was one

of the parsons. Patrick met his uncle at his carriage
when he arrived at the courthouse and asked him if he
wouldn't turn his carriage around.

He had never spoken in public, Patrick explained,
and his uncle's presence would overawe him. Besides,
he might say something about the parsons that his
uncle wouldn't like. So wouldn't he please just go
home? His uncle complied.

But Patrick couldn't ask the same of his father. Colonel John Henry was the presiding justice of the day and all through the trial he'd be sitting on a bench in front of the courtroom, right before Patrick's eyes.

Actually Colonel Henry was as uneasy as his son. He prayed that Patrick, who had failed in so many things, would not be an embarrassment today. But when Patrick stood up to argue the case, he was stooped, awkward, unable to look at the audience. When he spoke, he fumbled for words, halted, started sentences, stopped them as if he'd forgotten where he was going.

Colonel Henry sank down in his chair. He studied his hands. He looked out the window. Patrick's friends in the courtroom stared at the floor. What on earth had Patrick done with his voice, they asked themselves. Why didn't he *send* it?

Then all at once something seemed to come over Patrick. He stopped thinking about the people in the courtroom and about his father looking out the window and he began thinking about the King of England and how he could, if he wanted, change the character of the cheerful, independent world that Patrick lived in. Patrick Henry straightened up, he threw back his head, and sent his voice out in anger. How did the king know how much Virginians could pay their parsons? he asked. What right did he have to interfere? Patrick was rolling his words out now like his Uncle Langloo. He was doing things with his voice that he had never

known he could do—lowering it, raising it not only to fit his emotions but in such a way as to stir the emotions of everyone in the courtroom. The crowd sat transfixed. So did Colonel Henry. And why not? Here was Patrick Henry, a poor country lawyer, turning himself into an orator right before their eyes.

He talked for an hour. What about the parsons? he asked. Were they feeding the hungry and clothing the naked as the Scriptures told them to? No, he said. They were getting the king's permission to grab the last hoecake from the honest farmer, to take the milk cow from the poor widow.

When Patrick had finished, the jury took just five minutes to reach a decision. They could not deny the parsons all damages since a previous court had ruled they had to be paid something, but after hearing Patrick, they allowed the parsons so much less than they had asked for that the parsons demanded a retrial. They were refused.

The people in the courthouse were beside themselves with excitement at Patrick's success. As soon as court was adjourned, they raised him to their shoulders and carried him around the courtyard, hip-hip-hooraying him all the while. As for Colonel Henry, when asked about his son's performance, he smiled. He'd been pleasantly surprised, he said.

It was a good thing for America, as it turned out, that Patrick Henry became an orator at the same time that England was unfolding her new plan. Taxation was England's next step. Although Americans had always managed their own money, suddenly in 1765 the English government, without any kind of by-your-leave from America, slapped down a stamp tax on the colonies. It had provisions for taxing 55 separate items and Patrick Henry was ready to fight every one of them.

On May 29th, 1765, Patrick became twenty-nine years old. He and Sarah had four children now and were living in a four-room house on top of a hill in Louisa County. And on the 29th of May, what was he doing?

Well, he was bawling out the king again. He had become a member of the House of Burgesses, Virginia's governing body, only nine days before and now he was standing up in his buckskin breeches before the finest men of Virginia, using such bold language that at one point there was a cry of "Treason!" But Patrick went right on reeling off resolutions. Later these resolutions were printed and sent out through the colonies, giving other Americans courage to oppose the taxation. Indeed, there was so much opposition to the Stamp Tax that after a year the king repealed it.

But England did not give up the idea of taxation nor did Patrick give up talking. In 1773, when England decided to enforce a tax on tea, Patrick went right to the floor of the House. He was so spellbinding that in the middle of one speech the spectators rushed from the gallery to the cupola of the capitol to pull down the English flag. The members of the House, noticing the commotion, thought there was a fire and ran for safety.

Patrick and Sarah had six children now and were
back in Hanover County in an eighteen-room house set
on a thousand acres. Patrick was a public figure. When
he went out, he wore a black suit or perhaps his
peach-blossom-colored one, silver buckled shoes, and
a tie wig which he was said to twirl around his head
when he was excited.

Yet his private life contained much sadness. After the

birth of their sixth child, Sarah lost her mind, turning on her husband and her own children in such a way that until she died in 1775 she had to be confined to her room. Unfortunately the years of Sarah's illness were also the critical years for the country and again and again Patrick was obliged to leave home. During one of her most severe spells he was with George Washington in Philadelphia, attending the Continental Congress.

On March 23rd, 1775, just a few weeks after Sarah's death, Patrick delivered his most famous speech at St. John's Church in Richmond, Virginia. By this time everyone knew who Mr. Henry was; they had all heard of his passion for liberty and of the extraordinary quality of his voice. There were those who swore that Patrick Henry could not even announce that it was a cold evening without inspiring awe. So of course on March 23rd St. John's Church was filled to overflowing

—people standing in the aisles, in doorways, sitting on window ledges.

Patrick Henry was angry not only at the king who was disregarding America's petitions, insisting on taxation, and preparing for war, but he was also angry at those people in America who still wanted to be friendly to the king and keep peace. Patrick stood up and pushed his

glasses back on his head which was what he did when he was ready to use his fighting words.

"Gentlemen may cry peace, peace," he thundered, "but there is no peace . . . Is life so dear or peace so sweet, as to be purchased at the price of chains and slavery?" Patrick bowed his body and locked his hands together as if he, himself, were in chains. Then suddenly he raised his chained hands over his head.

"Forbid it, Almighty God!" he cried. "I know not what course others may take but as for me—" Patrick dropped his arms, threw back his body and strained against his imaginary chains until the tendons of his neck stood out like whipcords and the chains seemed to break. Then he raised his right hand in which he held an ivory letter opener. "As for me," he cried, "give me liberty or give me death!" And he plunged the letter opener in such a way it looked as if he were plunging it into his heart.

The crowd went wild with excitement. One man, leaning over the balcony, was so aroused that he forgot where he was and spit tobacco juice into the audience below. Another man jumped down from the window ledge and declared that when he died, he wanted to be buried on the very spot that Patrick Henry had delivered those words. (And so he was, 25 years later.)

The next year war came and Virginia volunteers marched off to battle with *Liberty or Death* embroidered on their shirtfronts. As for Patrick Henry, the people elected him governor.

On May 29th, 1777, he was elected for the second time. He was forty-one years old now, living in the luxurious palace where the royal governors had lived for 55 years. And he was busy, so busy that if a nice spring day came along, he wouldn't even have heard a redbird call.

Indeed, he scarcely had time for his private life, yet he did have one rather important matter to attend to. Patrick wanted to marry twenty-one-year-old Dorothea Dandridge of Hanover County—that is, if he could find the time. Between his election as governor and his inauguration, he managed to take a week off and squeeze in some courting. On October 7th he traveled again to Hanover County, married Dorothea on the 9th, and was back in Williamsburg on the 15th.

Fortunately he was back in time to hear the good news that the American army had defeated the English at Saratoga, New York. This was the first major victory for the Americans, the turning point of the war, and so of course throughout the land the people celebrated. In Williamsburg there was a Grand Illumination: every window in every house, including the many windows of the Governor's Palace, held a lighted candle and in the cupola of the palace a lantern blazed. Bells rang, soldiers paraded, drums beat, people partied, danced, shouted, and sang. Walter Lenox, the wigmaker, celebrated so hard that he imagined he was a cannon. Boom-booming and bang-banging all night, he insisted that cannons did not go to bed.

Altogether Patrick served as governor five times. He was a good governor but he has been remembered best as an orator. He spoke less often now but once after the war he stepped to the speakers' platform and on and off for two weeks he stayed there. The issue was the Constitution of the United States. Patrick was against it. He had always imagined that after Americans had disposed of England, they would settle down, state by state, to the cheerful, independent world he had known as a boy. There would, of course, be a federal government but not one with the powers that this Constitution proposed. The individual and his rights would be of first importance, but in this Constitution freedom of speech was not even mentioned, or freedom of religion or other freedoms that Patrick regarded so highly. So in 1788 when Virginia held a convention to decide whether to approve the Constitution, Patrick traveled to Richmond to speak his piece.

Several times he made 3 speeches in one day; once

he made 5; once he made 8. One day he spoke all day long and people listened to him with the same excitement as they always had. His eyes still held that famous "Patrick flash," they said, and when he held up his arms, he seemed to be covering the whole room. (A diamond ring blazed from one of the fingers.) But impressed as the people were, more voted for the Constitution than against it and it was eventually approved by all the states. Still, Patrick's marathon speaking had an effect. After the new government was formed, a Bill of Rights was added to the Constitution with all those freedoms that Patrick had fought for.

On May 29th, 1796, Patrick Henry was 60 years old. He had retired from public life and though he often grumbled about the government, his private world was as cheerful as any and more comfortable than most. He had lived many places over the years and had accumulated thousands of acres scattered throughout the state. And he was proud of those acres. More proud, his friends claimed, than of his public career—perhaps even a bit vain. After all, people had once doubted if he'd ever make a living and here he was, along with George Washington, one of the largest landholders in the state. And how had he done it? Thomas Jefferson said he had done it just by the use of his tongue. Not a good speaker himself and never impressed by Patrick's mental abilities, Mr. Jefferson added: Patrick Henry was *all* tongue; he was nothing but tongue.

Patrick spent his last years at his favorite piece of property, Red Hill, in the western part of the state. He had 29,000 acres, a river, a woods, and a story and a half house to which he added a low-ceilinged sleeping room so he could lie in bed and listen to the rain on the roof. People bragged that Patrick could manage much of his estate without even moving. All he had to do was to stand under the locust tree in front of his house and "send" out his voice to direct field workers half a mile or more away.

He lived just as he liked to live—knee-deep in dogs and children. Dorothea added eleven children to the family and, of course, by this time there were grandchildren too. Patrick encouraged them all to go barefoot. He didn't like to see children in shoes until they were six or seven years old and he believed that, if possible, they should avoid the inside of a schoolhouse until they were twelve. Nature, itself, was the best teacher, he said, and in his old age, as in his younger years, he took every opportunity to enjoy it. Come a nice spring day and Patrick Henry might be off to the

woods, one child in the saddle before him and one be-
hind. Or he might be walking down to the river, trailed
by a string of children and dogs. Or again he might be
simply sitting in the shade of the huge old orange osage
tree that spread its branches over most of the front
lawn. He'd have some children with him, of course; his
fiddle would be handy, and beside him there would be
a bucket of cool spring water with a gourd for drinking.

And if a redbird called—well, Patrick Henry would
be ready for it. He'd just lean back in his chair and
answer.

Notes from the Author

On some of the pages of this book, readers may want additional information.

Page

8   The Totopotomoy was the creek that Patrick used. It was named for an Indian king who had been killed helping white settlers fight other Indians.

14   For the last five years of his education, Patrick, along with a dozen or more boys, went to school to his father, one of the few educated men in the county. He studied Latin, a little Greek, mathematics, and history (which he liked best).

22   Most of Patrick's cases were debt cases but he did represent his cousin, John Winston, when he accused a neighbor of calling him a hog stealer.

24   One reason that England started to tax America was that it had just finished fighting the long French and Indian war on American soil and was badly in debt. The English thought Americans should help pay that debt but Americans said they had fought the war too and had their own troubles.

44   Patrick Henry   was offered various positions in the federal government but refused them all.

47   He died on June 6, 1799.